This book belongs to the amazing, resilient:

_____

D1530107

Acknowledgements

I am so grateful and truly blessed for having received such guidance and support from the leadership of Reconnect for Resilience™. I have gained an unimaginable amount of knowledge and insight through the teachings of this curriculum. I am equally thankful for the opportunities and encouragement they have provided for me to share this gift with other child life specialists, medical staff, children and caregivers. For more information on the Reconnect for Resilience™ trainings please visit: www.resourcesforresilience.com

Thank you, Preston, for reminding me to breathe.

Copyright 2019 Julian Cate.
All rights reserved. No part of this document may be reproduced or transmitted in any form or by any means, electronic, mechanical, photocopying, recording, or otherwise, without prior written permission of Julian Cate.
ISBN: 9781072092186
Independently published

"Open different doors, you may find a <u>YOU</u> there that you never knew was yours.
Anything can happen."
-Mary Poppins

What does it mean to be resilient?

Resiliency is a strength found inside <u>all of us</u>. You can't see it or touch it, but it is there. This strength inside of us helps to overcome things in our lives that are hard. Being resilient can help us feel more comfortable again inside our bodies after something stressful has happened. If resiliency was something you could see or touch, it might be like a soft and sturdy blanket, wrapping around us to keep us warm and safe.

Some people are more resilient than others, but the GOOD NEWS is we can always learn new ways to handle the hard things in life so we can become more resilient and more comfortable inside our bodies!

<u>Caregiver Led Activity</u>: Decorate the outside of an empty shoebox or tissue box with markers, stickers, magazine clippings, etc. Encourage the child to decorate the box to reflect their style and interests. This represents the part of us that people can see, like our style of clothes, hair, make-up, and even our behavior. Ask the child to write down on strips of paper what strengths and good qualities they possess. What makes them resilient? What are good things about them that nobody else sees? Place the pieces of paper inside the box. This represents the good qualities about us that people cannot see or touch, such as kindness, compassion, or resiliency.

This book can help us understand how our brains and bodies <u>take care</u> of stress and anxiety when life overwhelms us. Just like we use <u>tools</u> to fix a broken car engine or a wobbly chair leg, we use <u>resiliency tools</u> to fix and adjust how we handle stress inside our bodies.

Can you think about a time in your life when you overcame something hard or scary? Write down what you did to get through this difficult time.

_____

_____

_____

_____

Think about this moment when you knew you were going to be OK. As you think about this moment, what feelings inside your body do you notice?

THIS IS IMPORTANT!

With patience and practice, these tools help us to press the **"brake pedal"** of our nervous system <u>just enough</u> to calm things down inside of us.

<u>AND...</u>

just like there are always new roads being built for cities and highways, our brains begin building NEW ROADS that help our tools work better and faster.

Resiliency tools are all about learning how to <u>communicate</u> to the nervous system inside our bodies.

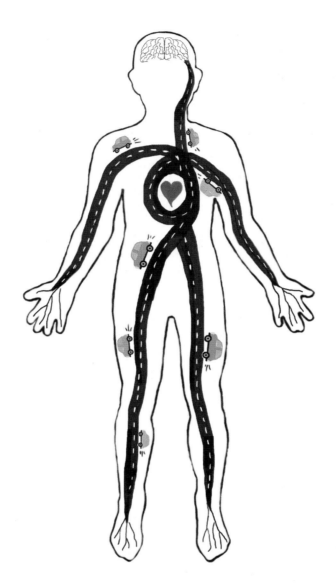

Our nervous system is like a **<u>busy highway</u>** inside of us that connects our brains and bodies together. Along this highway, there are millions of cars traveling up and down the roads. These cars send and receive messages about what is happening in and around us.

When we learn something new, like how to ride a bike, a new road is built. The more we practice something, the bigger and wider the road becomes, and the more traffic it can handle.

THINK ABOUT IT THIS WAY:

Each car has a gas pedal and a brake pedal. When we need to pay attention to something that might be important, scary or dangerous, our cars press the gas pedal (car driving uphill).

For example: a fire drill at school, our turn at bat in a baseball game, or when we are getting a shot at the doctors' office. Our heartbeat speeds up, the pupils in our eyes get bigger, and our muscles tighten up. **This is normal!** We really need our gas pedal throughout the day. It's what gets our bodies prepared to handle stress or find safety.

Once the stress or worry has passed, and our bodies feel safe again, our nervous system presses the brake pedal (car driving downhill). The brake pedal helps our bodies to balance back out again. This gas and brake pedal work back and forth all day long inside of us.

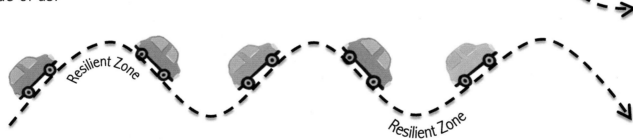

When we are handling stress, and our bodies can balance back out again, this is called being in our **resilient zone**.

Caregiver Led Activity: Draw a wavy line onto paper or in the sand. Ask the child to slowly and repeatedly trace over the line with their finger or a small car. As they trace, encourage them to identify a time when they felt like they were in their resilient zone. As they describe that moment, ask them to notice what their body feels like on the inside.

Sometimes...

our **gas pedal** gets pressed <u>too hard</u>, or for <u>too long</u>. If this happens, our bodies can feel out of balance. We can feel nervous, anxious or scared, and we don't really know why.

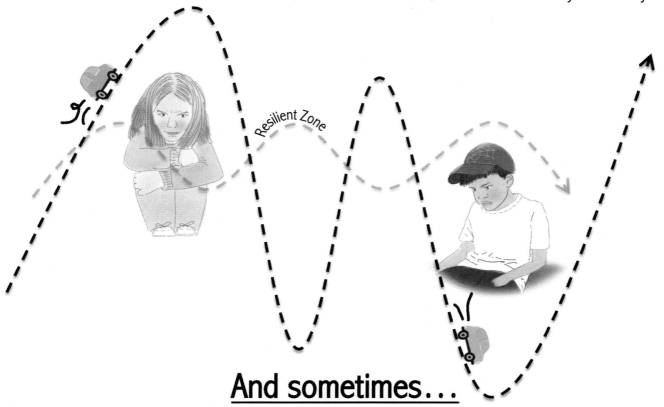

And sometimes...

our **brake pedal** can get pushed <u>too hard</u>, or for <u>too long</u>. This can also cause us to feel out of balance. We don't feel like being with friends or family very much, or we may feel really sad and tired a lot.

<u>Caregiver Led Activity:</u> Using the same wavy line as before on page 7, ask the child to slowly and repeatedly trace the line with their finger or small car. As they trace, encourage the child to identify a time when they felt their gas or brake pedal working too much. As they describe that moment, ask them to notice what their body feels like on the inside. If the child becomes upset by this experience, repeat the activity on page 7 to help them feel more balanced again.

<u>Most of the time...</u>

we react to stress with <u>**LOTS**</u> of gas pedal action. To help our bodies settle back down, we need to press the brake pedal of our nervous system.

<u>DID YOU KNOW?</u>

Our bodies communicate with us all of the time!

But <u>HOW</u> our bodies communicate is different than how we communicate with each other. We use <u>words</u> to communicate. Our bodies communicate using the highway inside of us.

The cars send messages of **<u>physical feelings</u>** to certain parts of our bodies. These feelings could be "butterflies in our tummy" if we are nervous, a warm face if we feel embarrassed, or a fluttery feeling in our chest if we are excited.

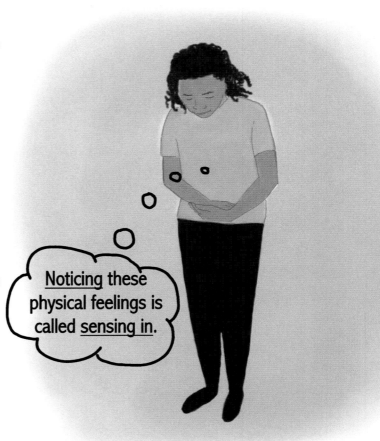

Noticing these physical feelings is called <u>sensing in</u>.

<u>**Caregiver Led Activity:**</u> Using playdough or a small soft toy, have the child squeeze the object in their hand really hard for 5-10 seconds. Repeat one or two more times. When finished, ask the child to notice what their hand feels like. For example, is their hand warm, cool, tingly, or heavy? Can they notice what the muscles in their hand feel like, or how fast or slow their heart is beating? By noticing these types of feelings, the child is learning how to pay attention to their body's communication style.

There are 2 kinds of feelings:
<u>Emotional</u> and <u>Physical</u>

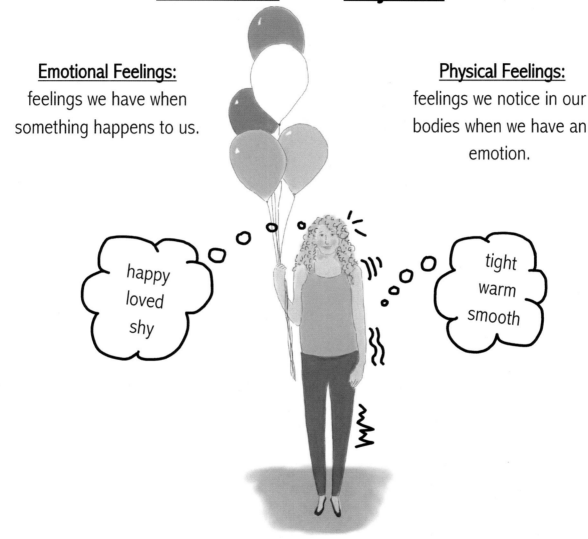

<u>Emotional Feelings:</u>
feelings we have when something happens to us.

<u>Physical Feelings:</u>
feelings we notice in our bodies when we have an emotion.

happy
loved
shy

tight
warm
smooth

<u>Caregiver Led Activity:</u> Draw the child's body outline onto a large sheet of paper or use a generic print-out. Ask the child to identify certain physical feelings they experience with different emotions (i.e. "When I am scared, I feel my chest getting tight"). Using the body outline, ask them to write or draw where in their body they notice these feelings.

Draw a line to connect
your <u>emotional</u> feelings to your <u>physical</u> feelings

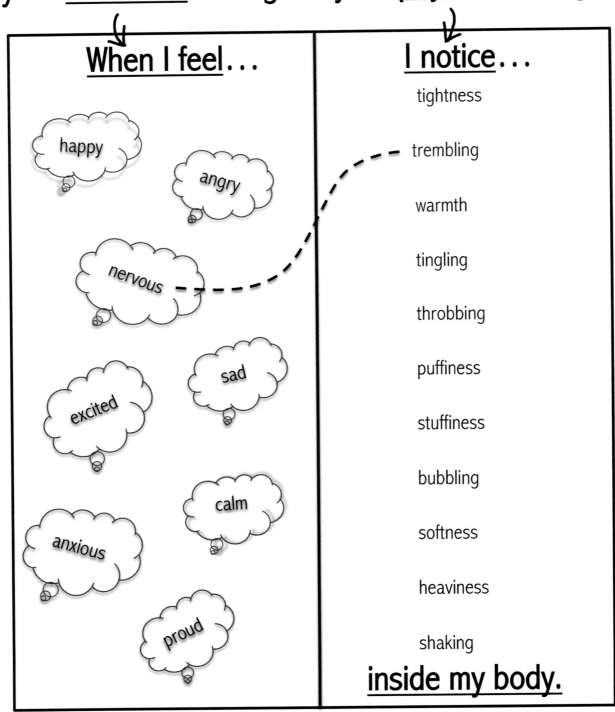

<u>When I feel</u>...	<u>I notice</u>...
happy	tightness
angry	trembling
nervous	warmth
	tingling
	throbbing
excited	puffiness
sad	stuffiness
	bubbling
calm	softness
anxious	heaviness
proud	shaking
	<u>inside my body.</u>

When we are feeling joyful, happy, or calm, we may notice physical feelings inside our bodies that are **comfortable** and feel **balanced**.

settled

loose

warm

bubbly

calm

smooth

still

Some physical feelings can seem **uncomfortable** and **unbalanced**. We may notice these feelings in our bodies when we are grumpy, scared or angry.

shaky

tight

light headed

short of breath

sweaty

trembling

jumpy

<u>Now, imagine our hand as a brain in 3 parts:</u>

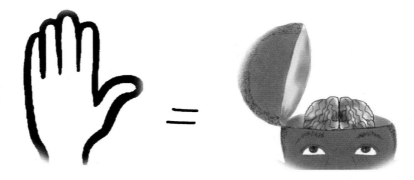

By making a fist, with the thumb tucked inside, we can learn about the brain and what happens to us when we feel stressed and anxious.

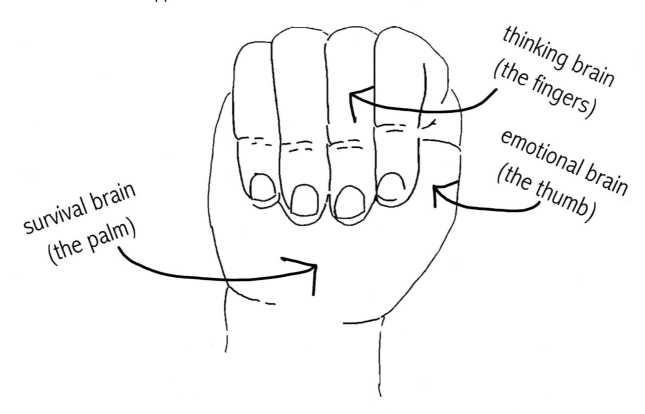

thinking brain (the fingers)

emotional brain (the thumb)

survival brain (the palm)

*Siegel, D.J. (1999) Full citation is located in back of book

Our palm represents the "survival brain".

The survival part of the brain controls all of the things that happen automatically inside our bodies that help us SURVIVE. Things like our heartbeat, breathing, and digestion. The **physical feelings** that happen inside our bodies when we get nervous, scared, angry, sad, happy, and excited are also controlled by this part of the brain.

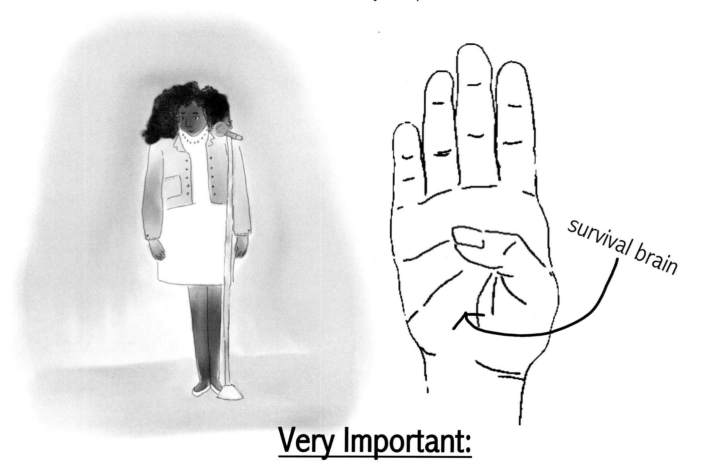

survival brain

Very Important:

The survival brain also controls what happens inside our bodies when we want to run away from something scary, fight someone who has made us mad, or freeze up like a statue when we get so afraid that we can't run away or fight. When those feelings control our bodies, it's called **"fight, flight or freeze"**.

"fight, flight or freeze"

When we are really scared, our bodies go into the "fight, flight or freeze" response. We <u>lose control</u> of how we react to the fear we are experiencing.

Was there ever a time when you felt really angry, scared, or sad about something?

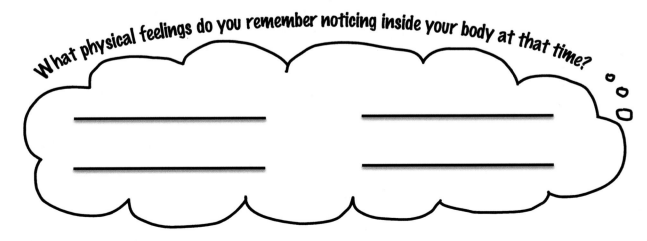

What physical feelings do you remember noticing inside your body at that time?

Now, point to your thumb. This represents the
"<u>emotional brain</u>"

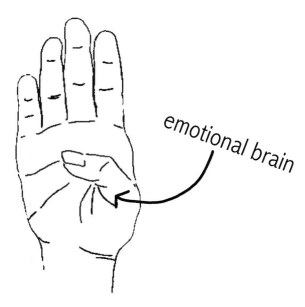

emotional brain

The emotional brain controls all of our emotions. It helps us to form friendships, feel connected to people we love (attachment), and <u>understand</u> how others may be feeling (empathy). This is also where our memories are kept.

Write about a memory of when you felt really **connected** to someone you love.

_____

_____

_____

_____

_____

_____

_____

_____

What physical feelings do you notice when you really think about this memory?

NOW...

Write about a memory of when you felt **empathy** for someone else.

_____

_____

_____

_____

_____

_____

_____

_____

What physical feelings do you notice when you really think about this memory?

The "guard dog" of the brain:

Part of the emotional brain is called the <u>amygdala</u> (a-mig-duh-la). The amygdala is like a friendly **guard dog** that keeps watch all the time, checking for safety, even when we are sleeping. If something seems unsafe, the guard dog BARKS! The barking alerts us to <u>jump into action</u> (car driving up hill).

If we touch a hot stove, "BARK! BARK! BARK!..."
we pull our hand away.
If we see a snake on the ground, "BARK! BARK! BARK!..."
we jump back.
Can you think of another example?

☐ Sometimes, our guard dog barks at things that <u>seem</u> scary and unsafe even when there is <u>no danger</u>!

getting a flu shot!   reading in front of the class

a friend sneaking up on you

Now, fold the fingers over to make a fist, but keep your guard dog tucked inside. The last part of the brain, where our fingers are, is called the

"thinking brain"

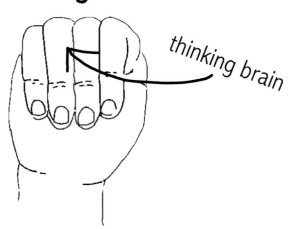

thinking brain

Our thinking brain allows us to think clearly and make good decisions for ourselves and others around us. In this position, our brain is able to concentrate for a test, solve a conflict, be creative and imaginative, or even figure out...

where in the world I left my jacket!

Resilient Zone

Using one of the experiences from page 17, fill in the boxes below.

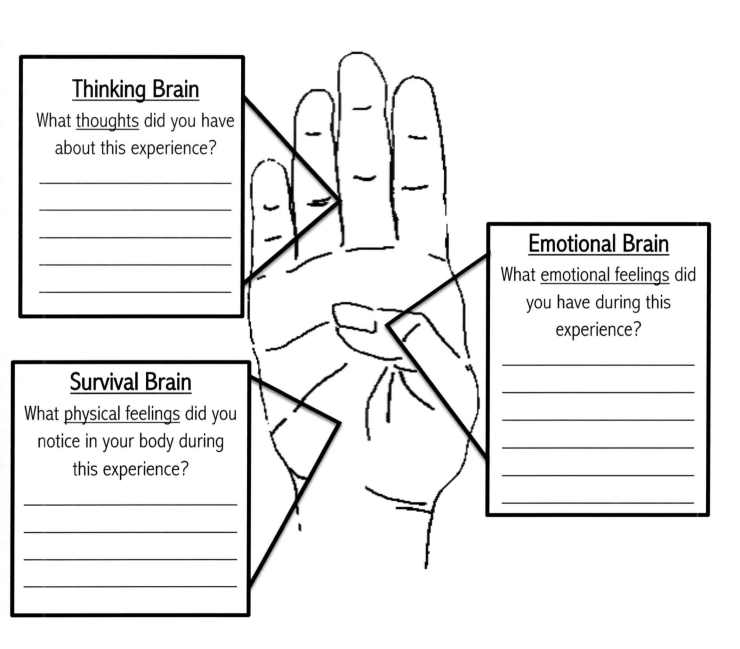

Thinking Brain
What <u>thoughts</u> did you have about this experience?

_____

_____

_____

_____

_____

Emotional Brain
What <u>emotional feelings</u> did you have during this experience?

_____

_____

_____

_____

_____

_____

_____

Survival Brain
What <u>physical feelings</u> did you notice in your body during this experience?

_____

_____

_____

_____

Everyone experiences stress and worry. If you sometimes feel so **ANGRY** that you think you are going to **SNAP**, then you are not alone! When something happens to us that causes a really big stress, our guard dog begins to bark. If the dog barks loud enough or long enough, our thinking brain can "flip its lid" like this:

When our thinking brain "flips its lid", our nervous system slams down on the gas pedal or brake pedal. We suddenly cannot think clearly or make good choices. Instead, our **survival brain** takes over, sending out physical feelings in our body that make us want to fight, scream, cry or run away.

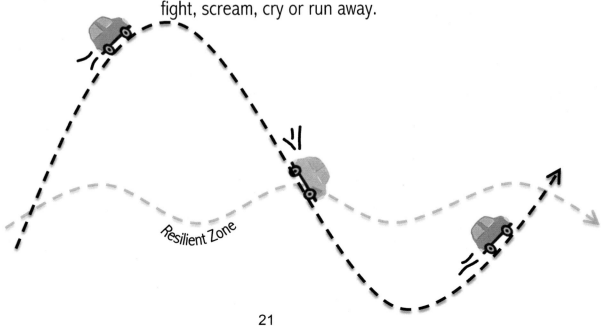

Resilient Zone

YOU MIGHT BE WONDERING...

"What can I do when I feel so <u>overwhelmed</u> with my emotions that I can't seem to get my thinking brain to settle back down?"

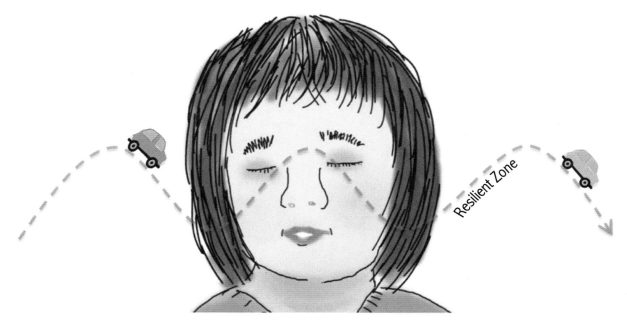

Resilient Zone

FIRST and MOST IMPORTANT:

When our "lid is flipped", the best way to get back into our resilient zone is to communicate directly to the **survival brain** using the language it <u>understands</u> the best.

Remember:

Our survival brain has taken over, so it is helpful to know how to talk to it so it can listen!

The survival brain does not use language like Spanish or English.

The language it uses to communicate is the
language of physical feelings!

Here are 6 tools that you can learn and practice to help quiet your survival brain, and help get your thinking brain to settle down:

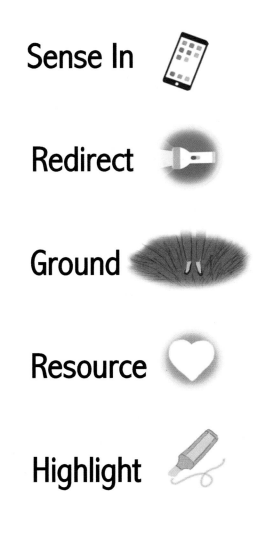

Sense In

Redirect

Ground

Resource

Highlight

Rapid Reset

Not all of the tools are a good fit for everyone. As you practice, you will be able to figure out which ones work best for <u>YOU</u>.

Sense In

The Sense In tool is helpful in all moments of your day. It is the <u>first</u> tool to learn about because it is a part of all the other tools!

Just like receiving a text message on your phone, this tool is all about noticing that your body is communicating a message of safety, comfort or danger.

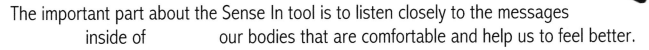

The important part about the Sense In tool is to listen closely to the messages inside of our bodies that are comfortable and help us to feel better.

With practice, Sensing In helps us to create different pathways in our brains that stay **AWAY** from uncomfortable feelings in our bodies like tight muscles, fast heartbeat, trembling hands, or aching stomach.

Instead, Sensing In helps us build <u>new pathways</u> in our brains that allow us to handle stress and anxiety in a healthier way.

Sense In will naturally become a part of your everyday life as you practice. Over time, you will learn how to press the **brake pedal** of your nervous system all on your own when you are feeling uncomfortable with worry.

Let's Practice

Take your hands and rub them together really fast. Keep going for at least 30 seconds. Now <u>stop</u>. What do your hands feel like? What physical feelings do you notice on the inside and outside of your hands? Write them down here if you choose to:

_____   _____

_____   _____

Another way to practice is to focus your thoughts on the inside of your body.
Focus your thoughts on your heartbeat. How fast or slow is it? Can you feel the beats inside your chest? Or, can you hear your heart beating?

Now,

focus your thoughts onto your breathing. How fast or slow are you breathing? Can you feel your breath inside your nose and lungs? Can you hear your breath?

And finally,

focus your thoughts on your muscles. See if you can focus your attention on the muscles in your arms and legs. Are they tight or loose? Do they feel settled or do they have some energy inside of them?

Great job! Just simply paying attention to the way your body feels will help you to learn about what your body is communicating to you. If your heartbeat, breathing and muscles feel comfortable, then your body is telling you that you are safe and sound. You just pressed the **brake pedal** for your nervous system!

Redirect

The Redirect tool is helpful whenever you are feeling pain somewhere in your body, or if your body feels uncomfortable from being worried or scared.

When we are hurting, our attention wants to go immediately to that spot. This gives the pain more power and can make it stronger. The Redirect tool is like an 'I SPY' game inside our bodies. In this game, we are seeking out places that are more comfortable or pleasant. When we Redirect our attention AWAY from the pain, the pain becomes less powerful.

Let's Practice

Pretend that you have a very small flashlight inside of your body. With this flashlight, search all around inside yourself. Look for places that feel better than where your pain is.

Don't let your flashlight shine on the place that is bothering you. If it does, move your light away from that uncomfortable place.

Keep looking...

Seek out all of the places inside of you. Shine your light on the inside of your toes, your elbows, your ears, your shoulders.

Search for the place that feels the MOST comfortable. When you find this place, shine your flashlight in that spot for <u>as long as you can</u>.

Notice any comfortable feelings in that spot?

circle the ones you notice

smooth   cool   fuzzy

energized   calm

airy   still   settled

solid   bubbly   warm

_____   _____

_____

or add in your own

Remember

If your flashlight tries to sneak over to the place in your body that is bothering you, just move it back to where you want it.

After about 2 minutes, has your body begun to feel better? Has your pain eased up some, or even all the way? If so, <u>Great Job!</u> You just communicated to your survival brain using the language of physical feelings and helped yourself settle back down!

If not, try searching around some more with your light. Do the exercise a bit longer, or switch to another tool. This takes time at first. The more you practice, the easier it will be to do this exercise.

Ground

Grounding is helpful when your mind is zooming all around thinking of things that are upsetting or worrisome. It could be things that already happened, or things that are coming up. Our bodies can start to feel unbalanced and uncomfortable. When the barking dog starts up, it can help to practice grounding so that we can signal <u>safety</u> to our survival brain.

Let's Practice

First, find a comfortable position. If you are sitting, place your feet <u>flat</u> on the ground. If you are lying in bed, find a comfortable place for your feet and hands.

For a short time, pay attention to your heartbeat, breathing and muscles.

If you are standing, sitting or lying down, notice what is holding your body up. Is it the floor, a chair, or a bed? Whatever is supporting you right now, pay <u>close</u> attention to all of the parts of your body that are actually touching this item.

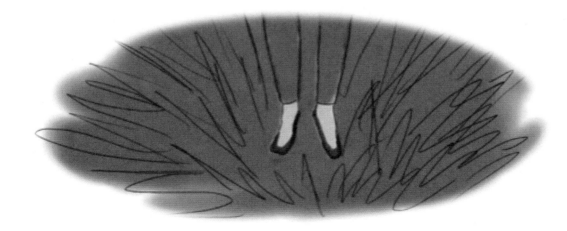

Notice the weight of your body as it is being held up by something that is stronger than you. See if you can find the part of your body that is being held up <u>the most</u>. If you are standing, notice what part of your feet are being held up the most by the ground. Is it your heels, the arches of your feet, or your big toes?

 Once you find that place that feels the most supported, keep your flashlight of attention on that one place for as long as you can.

What physical feelings do you notice in that one place?

When you are ready, move your attention back to your heartbeat, breathing and muscles. Does your heart feel calmer? Has your breathing settled down a bit? Have your muscles relaxed any? If so, then **<u>great job</u>!** You have just helped yourself press the **brake pedal** of your nervous system.

This may be difficult to do at first but keep practicing. We are not used to understanding this kind of language. With time, you will notice it getting easier.

Resource

Resourcing can be helpful during a stressful moment or when you feel down or frustrated about something. Resourcing can also be useful when your guard dog wants to keep barking even when you are <u>safe and sound</u>.

A resource is anything in your life that helps you <u>feel better</u>.

Let's Practice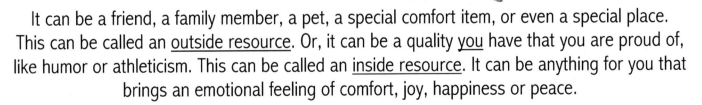

It can be a friend, a family member, a pet, a special comfort item, or even a special place. This can be called an <u>outside resource</u>. Or, it can be a quality <u>you</u> have that you are proud of, like humor or athleticism. This can be called an <u>inside resource</u>. It can be anything for you that brings an emotional feeling of comfort, joy, happiness or peace.

Write 3 of your resources here:

_____

_____

_____

Circle the resource that seems the most important for you
<u>in this moment.</u>

Write about a recent memory when you spent time with your resource. If it is an inside resource, describe a time when your special quality helped you feel important or valued. Describe lots of details of this memory. What sights, smells, and sounds were there? Who else was with you? What was the weather like that day? What decorations were on the walls?

_____

_____

_____

_____

_____

_____

_____

_____

_____

_____

_____

_____

_____

_____

_____

As you think about all of the details of your special memory, search around inside your body and notice <u>what is happening on the inside</u>. Where are the feelings inside your body that are pleasant, calm, or comfortable as you think about your resource? Once you find a place inside, try to keep your flashlight of attention there. What physical feelings do you notice in that spot? What does your heartbeat, breathing, and muscle tension feel like?

If you notice your body feeling better after you think of your resource, then you have just successfully pressed the **brake pedal** of your nervous system and helped your brain to settle back down again. <u>Great Job!</u>

 Highlight

The Highlight tool is helpful to us when something really overwhelming has happened in our lives. After the overwhelming moment has ended, our bodies can still experience <u>physical feelings</u> inside, like a nervous belly, a tight chest, racing thoughts, or shaky hands or legs. These feelings in our bodies can even last for <u>years</u> after the stressful event.

<u>You might be wondering...</u>

Why does our body <u>keep</u> on feeling this way long <u>after</u> a scary event has happened? Well, it's because our survival brain still thinks that it is in danger. To help it to settle back down, we need to communicate to it that we are safe and sound.

Let's Practice

Write about a time in your life when things were really hard. Maybe you experienced something scary like a sudden trip to the hospital, or maybe you have had someone you love die. Maybe someone has hurt you, or you saw someone else getting hurt. These things can cause really big feelings inside of us that can stay inside our bodies for a long time. Write about what has happened to you.

_____

_____

_____

_____

_____

_____

_____

_____

_____

_____

_____

_____

_____

_____

_____

_____

_____

As you tell the story of <u>your</u> scary, hard time, think about the moment when it all became better again. How did you <u>KNOW</u> that everything was going to be OK? Who came to help? In the highlighted section below, write about this exact moment?

_____

_____

_____

_____

_____

_____

_____

Read over this part again. As you think about that moment, <u>Sense In</u> to the physical feelings inside your body. Your body is using those physical feelings to communicate to you that you are safe and sound.

Rapid Reset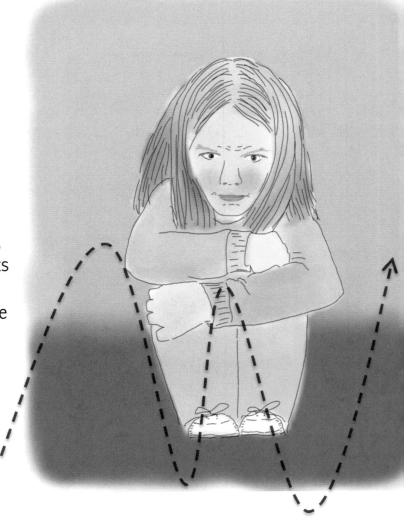

Rapid Reset tools are used when our "lid is flipped", and our nervous system is so out of balance that we need HELP right NOW!

Maybe you can't even think of trying to use some of the other tools because you are so **angry** and **frustrated** that nothing seems to work.

The cool thing about these Rapid Reset tools is there are several to choose from. When you start to understand how these tools work, you can even make up your own. The most important thing to remember is that when we are so uncomfortable with worry, and our thinking brain has totally "flipped its lid", our survival brain takes charge and starts bossing us around. It starts sending us messages to <u>fight</u> or <u>run away</u>, and these messages are very loud and hard to ignore.

The best way to get the survival brain to calm down is to communicate to it using the language of physical feelings. When we are able to understand our body's language, we can

press the brake pedal of our nervous system!

Rapid Reset tool #1: The 5 Senses

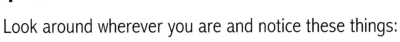

Look around wherever you are and notice these things:

5 Colors you see

4 Sounds you hear

3 Textures you feel

2 Smells you notice

1 Taste you notice

TAKE YOUR TIME.

Once you are done, pay attention to your heartbeat, breathing and muscle tension.
Do they feel a bit calmer?

Even if your body feels just a <u>little</u> bit better, you are on the right path!
Great Job!

You just pressed the **brake pedal** of your nervous system!

Rapid Reset tool #2: Wall Push

Find a <u>sturdy</u> wall that you can push against. You can use your hands or another part of your body like your shoulder or back. Push against it with all of your <u>power</u>. Lean into it and really push! Keep this up as long as you want to.

Pushing against a wall, using all of your muscles, helps your body get rid of the uncomfortable feelings trapped inside of you. This makes room for more of the comfortable ones.

Once you are done, notice any physical feelings on the inside of your body. What do your hands feel like after pushing against the wall? What do your feet feel like now? Pay attention to your heartbeat, breathing and muscle tension.

Notice <u>where</u> you feel better inside your body. Focusing on these places helps to get your nervous system back into balance.

Rapid Reset tool #3: Cold Drink of Water

Try drinking a glass of water or juice. It sounds so simple, and it really is. The trick is to notice what it feels like on the inside of your body as you drink. Notice the temperature of your drink. Notice what it feels like as it reaches your stomach. Pay attention to any comfortable physical feelings that you experience when you drink. As your drink settles inside of you, notice your heartbeat, breathing and muscle tension.

By paying <u>close</u> attention to these comfortable feelings, the brake pedal is pushed, and our bodies can begin to feel more settled and balanced.

Rapid Reset tool #4: Feel the Music

Listening to a favorite song is a wonderful way to help our nervous systems to settle down. No matter where we live in the world or how old we are, music is used to help bring a feeling of joy and comfort to our bodies. It is also used to help us to feel safe when we are scared or nervous.

While listening to a favorite song, notice what your heartbeat, muscles and breathing feels like. Listen to the <u>rhythm</u> of the music and the <u>words</u> being sung. Listen ALSO to the physical feelings in your body while the song is playing. If you like to sing along, then do it! Singing is also a great way to settle the nervous system. Singing encourages good breathing, which helps our brains to tell our bodies that we are safe and sound. Remember, noticing the physical feelings inside our bodies is called <u>Sensing In</u>. If your song also makes you think of a positive memory in your life, then <u>Sense In</u> to those feelings as you remember the details of this memory.

<u>Sensing In</u> as you listen is KEY. By doing that, we are <u>directly</u> communicating to our survival brain using language it understands. When we tell our survival brain that everything is safe, then the **brake pedal** is pushed, and our bodies can feel more balanced again.

My 'I AM' poem:

I am _____ AND _____
      (2 positive words that describe you)

I wonder _____
        (something you are curious about)

I hear _____ AND _____
      (2 sounds that you hear)

I want _____
      (a desire that you have)

I am _____ AND _____
      (the first line of the poem repeated)

I feel _____AND _____ on the inside of me
      (2 physical feelings you notice inside your body-example: heavy, light, shaky, smooth...)

I feel with my hands something _____
      (A texture you feel-example: soft, scratchy, smooth...)

I worry about _____
      (something that worries you)

I think about _____
      (name a resource for you)

I am _____ AND _____
      (the first line of the poem repeated)

I remember _____
      (a pleasant memory you have from a recent time in your life)

I say that _____
      (something you believe in)

I see _____
      (5 colors you see)

I hope _____
      (something you hope for)

I am _____ AND _____
      (the first line of the poem repeated)

Note to Caregivers:

When helping a child of any age cope with anxiety or trauma, caregivers can sometimes find themselves struggling to cope as well. If you have ever held your screaming child during immunizations, received yet another call from the school about your child's poor choices, or even experienced a death in the family, then you may know this all too well. It is important to give yourself lots of grace, and to know that there is no shame in how we can react sometimes to children's behavior. My hope is that this book can help shed some light on how we as human beings are hard-wired to respond in certain ways to stress and trauma that sometimes are not so socially pleasing. When our child, or a child we are caring for is hurting, or behaving in a threatening way, our brains send messages to our bodies that we, ourselves, are unsafe. Our reactions to these traumatic events may look like fighting, avoiding, or just plain freezing up in such fear that we don't appear to even care. If this has happened to you, please know this is an automatic response that can happen to all people in moments of actual danger and imagined danger. It's not your fault. Our bodies are designed to be like this. If you choose, I encourage you to take time yourself to practice these resiliency tools and techniques alongside your child. You will be better able to effectively help a child cope with anxiety and stress if you too are able to cope in a healthy way. As they say before takeoff in an airplane, '*if you are travelling with a child or someone who requires assistance, secure your mask on first, and then assist the other person*'.

Julian Cate is a Certified Child Life Specialist in Asheville, North Carolina. Her concentration is working with children and families in intensive care settings.

* Dr. Daniel J. Siegel's "Hand Model of the Brain," as first described in Siegel, D.J. (1999). *The developing mind: Toward a neurobiology of interpersonal experience (1st ed.)*. New York, NY: Guilford Press. © 1999 Mind Your Brain, Inc., and later depicted by visual image in Siegel, D.J. (2010). *Mindsight: The new science of personal transformation*. New York, NY: Random House. © 2010 Mind Your Brain, Inc. and Siegel, D.J. (2018). *Aware: The science and practice of presence*. New York, NY: Random House. © 2019 Mind Your Brain, Inc.

Made in the USA
Middletown, DE
31 December 2020

30508101R00027